An Un-Inheritance: New Law Of Succession

Sibongiseni Masengemu

Published by Sibongiseni Masengemu, 2025.

AN UN-INHERITANCE: NEW LAW OF SUCCESSION

First edition. September 3, 2025.

ISBN: 979-8232570866

Written by Sibongiseni Masengemu.

Table of Contents

Chapter 1: The Last Goodbye

The rain was a theatrical flourish, a final, dramatic gesture from the heavens as the casket was lowered into the Johannesburg earth. Thandie clutched her black umbrella with a white-knuckled grip, its ribs rattling against the insistent wind. She stood straight, her jaw set, a perfect monument of grief. Her parents, revered icons of the city's corporate elite, had been given a send-off befitting their status—a thousand mourners, a cathedral overflowing with flowers, and now, this perfectly manicured cemetery plot beside a granite angel.

On her left, Lungie trembled, a small, fragile thing swallowed by her mourning dress. She hadn't stopped crying since the phone call two days ago. Her sobs were small, pathetic sounds that Thandie found both endearing and deeply irritating. Lungie's hand found Jay's, and he squeezed it gently, his eyes fixed on the mound of red clay. Jay stood on Thandie's right, a stark contrast to her formal stillness. His tie was slightly askew, and he had a defiant tilt to his head, as if challenging the very act of burying his parents. He was an artist, a creator, and this finality was a brutal, physical thing he couldn't paint away.

Thandie glanced at him, a flicker of concern in her guarded expression. She knew he had barely spoken a word since their arrival, retreating into the silent fortress he had built for himself over the years. This was his way of grieving, she knew. While she meticulously planned every detail of the funeral—the eulogies, the floral arrangements, the catering—Jay had gone for a long, aimless drive, and Lungie had simply wept. They were a trio of mismatched parts, held together only by a name and the shared, echoing emptiness of a now-silent home.

As the ceremony concluded, Mr. Van Zyl, their parents' long-time lawyer, approached them. His face, usually a mask of practiced professionalism, was etched with an unfamiliar sorrow.

“My sincerest condolences,” he said, his voice a low rumble. “Your parents were... remarkable people.”

Thandie nodded, muttering a practiced thank you. She looked past him, towards the waiting procession of luxury cars. The world was watching, and she had a duty to perform. They were the children of titans, and they would not crumble in public.

“I have scheduled a meeting for tomorrow morning, at ten,” Mr. Van Zyl continued, his gaze shifting between the three of them, a hint of something unreadable in his eyes. “We need to discuss the estate. It's a formality, of course.”

Jay finally looked up, his expression a tight, hard line. "A formality?" he scoffed.

Lungie flinched. Thandie shot Jay a withering glance, a silent warning to behave. This was not the time. They were still in the public eye, still putting on a show. But as she watched her siblings, a cold, unsettling premonition took hold. They had always been defined by their parents' legacy, a golden, unshakable reality. Now, with a few words from a lawyer, that foundation was beginning to feel terrifyingly unstable. She had no idea how right she was.

Chapter 2: A Formality, of Course

The morning sun poured into their parents' study, illuminating the dust motes dancing in the air and the spines of countless leather-bound books. It was a room that smelled of old money, mahogany, and a faint, lingering scent of their father's pipe tobacco. The atmosphere, however, was far from golden. It was thick with a silence that had nothing to do with reverence and everything to do with simmering resentment.

Thandie sat in the chair her mother had used, her posture as rigid as ever. Jay paced by the large bay windows, his hands shoved deep into his pockets. Lungie was curled on the floor, clinging to the throw pillow she had just taken from her father's armchair, as if it could somehow comfort her. Mr. Van Zyl, the picture of professional composure, cleared his throat.

"I know this is difficult," he began, his voice softer than it had been at the funeral. "But as you know, there are a number of legal and financial matters that must be addressed."

Thandie nodded briskly. "We understand. Just tell us what we need to sign."

Mr. Van Zyl hesitated. He adjusted his glasses, a slow, deliberate movement. "I have searched the safe, the filing cabinets, and all digital archives. I have also spoken to your parents' assistants. I'm afraid... there is no will."

The words hung in the air like a sudden drop in temperature. Lungie's head snapped up. Jay stopped pacing, his body still, but his eyes blazing with a dangerous fire. Thandie's perfect composure cracked, just for a moment, a flicker of disbelief crossing her face before she masked it.

"What do you mean, no will?" Jay's voice was low, laced with venom. "My father was a meticulous man. He had a spreadsheet for his spreadsheets."

"He was meticulous, yes. That is why this is so puzzling," Mr. Van Zyl replied, his tone apologetic. "He revised his will every year on his birthday, but... he never signed the final version. It's as if he was waiting for something."

"Waiting for what? To die without a plan?" Thandie's voice was sharp with barely contained fury. "Do you have any idea what this means? The lawyers, the taxes, the... the mess? It will take years to sort out!"

"He left a letter," Mr. Van Zyl said, holding up a cream-colored envelope. "It's addressed to the three of you."

Jay snatched the letter, his fingers tearing into the sealed wax emblem. He unfolded the single sheet of paper, his eyes scanning the elegant script. As he read, his face drained of all color.

"Well, what does it say?" Thandie demanded.

Jay's hand trembled. He looked at his sisters, his expression a mixture of confusion and raw, unadulterated rage. "It says..." he stammered, his voice breaking. "It says the house, the companies, the cars... it's all gone. There's nothing left."

"That's impossible," Thandie whispered, a cold dread washing over her.

Jay crumpled the paper in his hand. "He sold everything. Every single thing. And he didn't leave us a dime. Not one single dime."

The silence that followed was a vacuum, sucking the very air out of the room. The tears that Lungie had been holding back finally broke free, but this time they were not of grief, but of pure, childish terror. A fight, venomous and vicious, was about to begin. The siblings, once united by their bloodline, were now three adversaries on a battlefield of shattered dreams.

Chapter 3: The First Fight

The vacuum of silence shattered. It was Lungie who broke first, a high-pitched wail of "How could they?!" that ripped through the air. Her fragile composure, already frayed, had finally disintegrated. She looked at the crumpled letter in Jay's hand as if it were a bomb, her face a mask of horrified betrayal.

"They did this to us! After everything we sacrificed for them, this is what we get?" she sobbed, sinking back onto the floor, clutching her throw pillow like a shield.

Jay's anger, however, was a slow-burning fuse that had just reached its core. He slammed his fist on the mahogany desk, the sound echoing through the study like a gunshot. "Sacrificed? What did you sacrifice, Lungie? Your trust fund was always there. The only one who sacrificed anything was me, trying to be a person they would actually be proud of instead of just another investment!"

Thandie's voice, a whip-crack of icy fury, cut through his outburst. "Oh, save the theatrics, Jay. This isn't about some emotional crisis. This is a complete disaster. Do you have any idea what this does to our standing in the community? The name, the legacy, everything they built—it's gone! Because of a foolish, sentimental mistake!"

"Sentimental? Thandie, are you even listening to yourself? Our parents just left us with nothing! Absolutely nothing! And you're worried about social standing?" Jay's voice rose, a raw, primal roar. He pointed a trembling finger at her. "You always were so worried about being the perfect daughter that you never saw what they were really like. This isn't a mistake—it's a slap in the face!"

"And you, Jay, are a child!" Thandie shot back, rising to her feet, her body a coiled spring of rage. "They gave you everything you ever wanted! An art studio, a car, your freedom—and what did you do with it? Nothing! You wasted it all, just like you're wasting this moment with your tantrums!"

Lungie, caught in the crossfire, screamed. "Stop! Just stop fighting! Don't you see? They're gone! And we're all we have left!"

But the words were lost in the storm of their resentment. The dam had broken. Years of unspoken jealousies, perceived slights, and simmering frustrations poured out. Thandie accused Jay of irresponsibility, and he accused her of being a heartless robot. They tore into each other's wounds with surgical precision, each word a shard of glass.

Lungie, overwhelmed, finally pushed herself to her feet and ran from the room, her cries echoing down the hall. Thandie and Jay didn't even notice. They stood facing each other, two bitter combatants on a battlefield of their parents' making. The house, once a symbol of their unity, now felt like a mausoleum, haunted by the ghosts of their past and the broken shards of their future.

Chapter 4: The Aftermath

Lungie ran until her lungs ached, her tear-streaked face a blotch of misery. She didn't stop until she was inside her old bedroom, a sanctuary frozen in time. The four-poster bed, the canopy of pink silk, the shelves filled with stuffed animals—it was all a museum to her past innocence. She collapsed on the plush rug, her body shaking with a different kind of pain than the grief she had felt yesterday. This pain was sharp, a betrayal that felt more intimate than death. They had always fought, but never like this. Their parents' death had not brought them together; it had torn them apart. She buried her face in her arms, letting out a raw, broken sob, feeling a loneliness she had never known, even in her parents' crowded home.

Meanwhile, Jay stood in the empty study, the silence a heavy blanket over his shoulders. The crumpled letter still lay on the desk, a testament to his fury. He picked it up and smoothed it out, reading the elegant, unfeeling script again. *They didn't leave us a dime.* The words were a brand on his soul. His anger had cooled into a cold, sharp determination. This wasn't just about money; it was about pride, about his very identity. He wasn't the aimless artist anymore; he was a son fighting for his legacy, for the recognition they had denied him even in death. His eyes scanned the room, looking for something, anything. His father was a man of patterns, of secrets buried in plain sight. There had to be something more. He would not stop until he found it.

In her own wing of the house, Thandie was no longer a monument of grief or a spring of rage. She was a machine. She had locked herself in her mother's immaculate home office and was on the phone with a new lawyer, a specialist in complex estate disputes. The first lawyer, Mr. Van Zyl, had been a family friend, a man who believed in formality and decorum. Thandie now knew that decorum had no place in this new reality. This was a war, and she was going to fight it with everything she had.

"I want you to dig into every one of my parents' accounts," she instructed, her voice calm and authoritative, the panic she felt a distant hum beneath her control. "I want to know where the money went. Every single cent. He couldn't have just... vanished it. The law requires a paper trail. Find it."

She hung up and stared at the framed photograph on the desk: her mother and father, smiling on a yacht in Monaco, a picture of effortless wealth. A wave of bitterness washed over her. It wasn't just about the money; it was about the humiliation. She had built her entire life on their name, their reputation, their fortune. Now, it was a house of cards, and she was watching it fall. She would not let that happen. She would find a way to get it all back, not just for herself, but for the legacy they had carelessly abandoned.

The once-united siblings were now three solitary islands, adrift in a sea of their parents' deceit. Lungie's world had shrunk to the four walls of her bedroom; Jay's had narrowed to the confines of his father's study; and Thandie's had expanded to the vast, complex world of corporate law. The fight was over, but the war had just begun.

Chapter 5: The First Move

The sun was setting, casting long, bruised shadows across the study as Jay methodically worked his way through his father's meticulously organized chaos. The man had a system for everything, from the labels on his file folders to the way he arranged his pens. There was no way he would have just vanished without a trace, without a contingency plan. Jay's earlier fury had given way to a quiet, cold concentration. He felt like a detective in his own life, searching for a clue that might unlock the reason for his parents' betrayal.

He ran his hands over the spines of the books, checking for loose bindings, then tapped along the paneling of the bookshelves, listening for a hollow sound. He moved to the desk, running his fingers along the ornate carvings of the dark wood. Just as he was about to give up, his thumb brushed against a small, almost invisible seam on the underside of a drawer. He pulled, and a small, narrow compartment slid open. Inside, nestled on a bed of faded velvet, was a single, old-fashioned brass key with a small leather tag attached. The tag was blank.

He pocketed the key, a surge of adrenaline pushing back the exhaustion he felt. This was it. This was the one thing his parents had hidden, and he knew, with a certainty that was both terrifying and exhilarating, that it was the key to everything.

Miles away, in a glass office tower with a panoramic view of the city, Thandie sat across from her new lawyer, Mr. Hendricks. He was a sleek, perfectly tailored man who didn't waste a single word. He listened to her account without a flicker of emotion, his fingers steepled beneath his chin.

“Thandie, your parents’ letter and the absence of a will make this a complicated case,” he stated, his voice a flat monotone. “On paper, there’s nothing to fight for. The assets were liquidated, and legally, the money is gone. We can certainly investigate, but it will be expensive, and the chances of a favorable outcome are low.”

“I don’t care about the cost,” Thandie replied, her voice steady and firm. “Find out where the money went. Every single cent. He was a businessman. He didn't just burn it. He invested it. And when he did, he created a paper trail. I want you to follow it. I want you to find the hidden asset. If it exists, I want it back. And I’ll pay whatever it takes.”

Mr. Hendricks gave a small, almost imperceptible nod. “As you wish. We'll begin digging today.”

Meanwhile, Lungie sat on the floor of her bedroom, cradling her phone in her hands. She couldn’t bring herself to call another lawyer. She didn't want to fight the way Thandie did, or search with the same desperate intensity as Jay. She wanted answers. She scrolled through her contacts and found the number she was looking for.

It was for Thembi, their parents’ long-time housekeeper, a woman who had practically raised all three of them. Thembi had been a source of comfort and quiet strength. Lungie hesitated, her thumb hovering over the call button. Thembi would know. She would have seen something. She had to. The phone rang once, then twice, before Thembi's warm, familiar voice answered, "Hello, my darling. Are you alright?"

Lungie's composure broke, and the words tumbled out in a single, desperate rush. “Thembi, I need your help. I think... I think our parents were hiding something.”

The three siblings were no longer simply grieving. They were now actively engaged in a silent war, each taking the first steps on a path that would either lead them back to each other or push them even farther apart. The fight for what was theirs had just begun, but they were not fighting on the same side, or even on the same battlefield.

Chapter 6: The Key and the Secret

Jay's hands trembled as he held the small brass key, the cold metal a stark contrast to the rush of heat in his veins. The study, once a place of silent authority, now felt like a puzzle box. He retraced his steps, his gaze sweeping over the polished wood and leather, looking for a hidden keyhole. He pulled on every book, tapped every panel, even ran his fingers over the intricate patterns of the oriental rug. There was no matching lock, no hidden compartment, nothing. His initial burst of adrenaline faded, replaced by a growing frustration. The key felt like a cruel joke, a taunt from the grave. What could it possibly be for? A safe deposit box? A locker at some obscure club? The possibilities were endless, and with each dead end, the weight of his task grew heavier. He sank into his father's worn leather chair, the silence of the room amplifying the frantic beat of his heart.

Meanwhile, a nervous tremor ran through Lungie's hands as she held her phone to her ear. Thembi's voice, a soft, soothing balm, had been a comfort, but now, a new fear was creeping in: the fear of what she might learn.

"Thembi, I'm so sorry to bother you with this," Lungie began, her voice a fragile whisper. "But... my parents... did they ever talk to you about anything? About money? Or... anything they were worried about?"

There was a long pause on the other end of the line, and Lungie was afraid Thembi would hang up. But then, Thembi's voice returned, low and cautious. "Your parents were very private people, my darling. They did not share their worries."

"But they must have said something!" Lungie insisted, a note of desperation creeping into her voice. "Anything at all. It's just... we're not okay. They left us with nothing, Thembi. Absolutely nothing."

Another, longer silence. Then, Thembi sighed, a sound heavy with years of unspoken secrets. "There was one thing. A place. Your mother used to go there when she was sad, or when she had a big decision to make. She called it her 'thinking place.' It was a small house. Not in the city. In the mountains. It was her secret."

Lungie sat up straight, her heart pounding. "A house? Where in the mountains?"

"I don't know the exact location," Thembi said. "But she had a key. A very special key. She would keep it in a small wooden box on her dresser. It was the only key she never let me clean."

A single, powerful word resonated in Lungie's mind: *key*. She knew Jay had found a key, and now Thembi was talking about one, too. Could it be the same one? Was this a clue for all of them, or just for Jay? She felt a sudden, desperate urge to call him, to share this new piece of information, but a fresh wave of hurt washed over her. After the fight, she wasn't sure she could trust him or Thandie with this. This was her secret now. Her chance to prove her worth.

She thanked Thembi and hung up, her mind racing. The key, the secret house, the blank tag. It was all a mystery, a trail of breadcrumbs left by her parents. Thandie was fighting a war of cold, hard facts, and Jay was trying to solve a puzzle. But she... she was looking for a secret, a place of sanctuary. And she was going to find it, on her own.

Chapter 7: The Secret House

Lungie didn't hesitate. She knew she couldn't tell Jay or Thandie. Not yet. Not after their vicious fight. This was her lead, her secret, her chance to prove she was more than just the flighty youngest sibling. She quietly packed a small bag, grabbed the car keys, and left the house without a word, a newfound purpose in her step. As she drove, the city's high-rises slowly gave way to rolling hills, then to the winding roads of the mountains. Thembi hadn't given her a specific location, only a feeling—a "place of peace." Lungie decided to trust her own intuition, taking roads that felt right, as if guided by an invisible hand.

Back at the house, Jay was on the verge of giving up. He had spent hours in the study, his frustration a raw, burning knot in his stomach. The brass key felt like a useless trinket, a mocking souvenir from a life that was now nothing more than a ghost. He had tried every lock in the house, even the ones on the liquor cabinet and the dusty old filing cabinets in the basement. Nothing. The blank leather tag offered no clue. He threw the key onto the desk in a fit of rage, the metallic clatter echoing in the silent room. He picked up his phone, thinking of calling his brother and sister, but the anger and bitterness of their last conversation were still too fresh. He was on his own.

In a downtown office, Thandie listened with a growing sense of dread as Mr. Hendricks spoke. He laid out a complex web of shell corporations and blind trusts, a fortress of legal documents designed to make tracking the money impossible. "Your parents were highly sophisticated, Thandie. They didn't just vanish the money; they made it disappear in a way that's nearly impossible to trace. We can send a legal notice, but it won't go anywhere."

"There has to be something," Thandie insisted, her voice tight. "My father would never leave himself exposed. There must be an asset, a contingency plan. A failsafe."

Mr. Hendricks sighed. "Perhaps. But a failsafe would be designed to be untraceable. We're working in the dark here."

The thought of losing everything—the status, the name, the life she had built—filled Thandie with a cold, desperate resolve. The money was a symbol, a proof of their legacy. And she would not let it vanish. She thanked her lawyer, her mind already racing, plotting her next move. The law might have a thousand loopholes, but she would find them all.

Meanwhile, Lungie's car rattled over a small, unpaved road, deep in the heart of a quiet forest. The road ended at a clearing, where a small, unassuming wooden cottage stood. It was a stark contrast to the sprawling family mansion, with its perfectly manicured lawns and grand architecture. This house was simple, rustic, and surrounded by a wild, untamed garden. A sense of peace, the very thing Thembi had described, settled over her. She got out of the car, her heart pounding with a mixture of fear and anticipation. She had found it. The question now was: What was inside?

Chapter 8: A Ghost of a Memory

The brass key felt heavy and cold in Lungie's hand as she approached the cottage door. The blank tag was a stark contrast to the intricate carvings on the key's bow, a silent mystery. A knot of anxiety tightened in her stomach. What if Thembi was wrong? What if this was just a place her mother came to be alone? Taking a deep breath, she slid the key into the lock. It turned with a satisfying, rusty click, and the door swung open with a slow creak, revealing a world frozen in time.

The air inside was cool and smelled of old paper and woodsmoke. Dust motes danced in the single beam of sunlight that cut through the window. The house was small, furnished simply but with immense care. A small bookshelf was filled with worn novels and gardening books. A single armchair sat beside a cold fireplace. On a simple wooden desk in the corner, a single, leather-bound journal lay open next to a stack of letters tied with twine. A note lay on top of the stack, in her mother's familiar, elegant handwriting.

Lungie approached the desk, her heart pounding a frantic rhythm against her ribs. She picked up the note. It was addressed to all three of them.

My Dearest Children,

If you are reading this, it means you have found our secret, our truth, and the path to what is truly yours. We did not leave a will because we could not. The money, as you know it, is gone. It was a burden, a crutch. Your father and I wanted you to learn to rely on your own strengths, not on a financial legacy. This house, and what is inside, is your inheritance. It is a lesson, a test, a key to a new life. And the real key to your inheritance lies in your ability to work together to find it. The truth, and the money, will be yours to share when you are ready. We love you more than you will ever know. Find each other. The rest will follow.

Tears streamed down Lungie's face as she sank into the armchair, the note clutched in her hand. The anger she had held onto for weeks dissolved into a profound, aching sadness. Her parents hadn't betrayed them; they had given them a puzzle, a final, desperate attempt to unite their fractured family. She looked at the journal on the desk, the letters tied with twine, and knew the truth was within reach.

Meanwhile, back at the mansion, Jay was at a dead end. He stared at the key on the desk, his mind replaying his father's words, his obsessive organization. The key wasn't for a lock; he had tried every one. It was a clue, a symbol. It was a key *to* something. He grabbed the blank leather tag and examined it under the light. It wasn't just blank; it was pristine, almost new, a recent addition. Why? He picked up the key again, and for the first time, he noticed the subtle engravings on its shaft: a small, almost invisible "M" and a set of coordinates. It wasn't the key to a lock; it was the key to a location. A ghost of a memory.

In her office, Thandie was hit with another blow. Her lawyer had just informed her that he was hitting a dead end. "The last remaining legal avenues are closed, Thandie. The money is lost to you, for good." The words hit her like a punch to the gut. The money was a symbol, a proof of their legacy. And it was gone.

Chapter 9: The Call

The note lay on the wooden desk, a fragile bridge between the past and a new, uncertain future. For a long moment, Lungie simply sat in the quiet cottage, absorbing the weight of her discovery. The anger that had fueled her journey had evaporated, replaced by a profound sense of sadness and a heavy responsibility. Her parents hadn't been cruel; they had been desperate. They had tried to leave them a legacy of unity, not just wealth.

Her eyes fell on the final sentence: *Find each other. The rest will follow.*

Her phone felt impossibly heavy in her hand. The last time she spoke to her siblings, they had torn each other apart, their words like daggers. Could they ever come back from that? But the message from her mother was clear. The key to everything wasn't in this house; it was in their ability to reconcile. With a deep, shaky breath, Lungie dialed Jay's number.

His voice, when he answered, was tired and defeated. "What?" he said, the single word a wall of exhaustion.

"Jay... it's me. I... I found something," Lungie said, her voice small. "You have to come here. To the cottage."

There was a pause on the line. "What cottage, Lungie? I'm busy. I've been running in circles for hours with this stupid key."

"The cottage Thembi told me about," she said, her voice gaining strength. "The one in the mountains. I found a note from Mom and Dad. And... they knew about the key, Jay. They knew about everything. You have to come."

There was a long silence, and Lungie could almost hear the gears turning in his head. The mention of the key had sparked something. "The mountains... the coordinates?" he mumbled to himself, more than to her. "Thembi... what is going on, Lungie?"

"Just come, please," she said. "Meet me here. I'll send you the address."

After hanging up with Jay, Lungie braced herself and called Thandie. The reception on the other end was even colder.

"I don't have time for this, Lungie," Thandie said, her voice sharp and brittle. "I'm in the middle of a legal nightmare you wouldn't understand. The money is gone."

"No, it's not," Lungie said, her voice firm. "They didn't just leave us with nothing, Thandie. They left us a test. A lesson. I found a note from them. I'm at a cottage in the mountains. Please, just come. Both of you. It's the only way we're going to get anything back."

For a moment, Lungie thought Thandie would just hang up. But the silence stretched, and she could sense Thandie's carefully constructed world of control crumbling. The reality of her failed legal battle, the finality of it, must have sunk in.

"Fine," Thandie said, the word clipped and cold. "Send me the address. I'll be there."

With her phone in her hand, Lungie stood in the center of the quiet room, a fragile sense of hope blooming in her chest. She had done the first part. She had found them. Now, all she could do was wait.

Chapter 10: The Unlocking

Jay arrived first. He had driven with a desperate, frantic energy, the coordinates on the key tag finally making sense. He pulled up to the small cottage, and a wave of disbelief washed over him. This was it? This was his father's big secret? It was nothing like the grand, imposing manor he had expected. He saw Lungie standing by the door, her face pale but her eyes full of a new, fierce resolve.

"Jay," she said, her voice a little shaky. "You came."

"The coordinates on the key matched the address," he said, holding up the brass trinket. "What is this place, Lungie?"

Before she could answer, a sleek black car crunched on the gravel behind them. Thandie emerged, her expensive suit a stark contrast to the rustic setting. She looked around with a skeptical, almost disgusted expression. "This is it? What is this nonsense, Lungie? I left a very important meeting for this."

The three of them stood in silence for a long moment, the unsaid words of their last fight hanging in the air between them like a thick fog. Thandie's jaw was set, Jay's shoulders were slumped in a mix of frustration and exhaustion, and Lungie just looked at them, a plea in her eyes.

"Mom and Dad left us a letter," Lungie finally said, her voice firm. "And they left it here, in the place where they came to be themselves. This is their legacy, Thandie. Not the money."

Without another word, she led them inside. Thandie's eyes immediately went to the simple furniture and the lack of grandeur. "Where is it? The will, the money, everything? Don't tell me this is the grand finale."

Lungie didn't respond. She just walked over to the desk and picked up the leather-bound journal and the note on top. "You need to read this," she said, her voice full of a quiet authority they had never heard from her before.

Jay and Thandie exchanged a glance, a silent, uneasy truce forming between them. They stood side-by-side as Lungie read the note aloud. Her voice trembled at first but grew stronger with each sentence, each word a punch to their gut. As she finished, the silence that followed was different from the one outside. This was a silence of profound shock and dawning realization.

Thandie's carefully constructed facade of control crumbled. "They... they put us through this... for a lesson?" she whispered, her voice raw with disbelief. "After everything? The law, the fight, the stress?"

Jay, who had been listening with his head bowed, finally looked up. He looked at the key in his hand, then at the blank tag, then at his siblings. "The coordinates weren't for a bank vault," he said, a ghost of a smile on his face. "It was for this place. The key to our legacy was never a physical thing. It was a person, a place... it was us."

Lungie looked at them, tears of relief and exhaustion streaming down her face. "They wanted us to be together," she said, her voice a soft, broken whisper. "They wanted us to be a family again."

For the first time since their parents' deaths, they looked at each other not as rivals, but as siblings, their shared grief and confusion finally overpowering their anger. The weight of their parents' message hung in the air, a burden and a gift. It was a key to a legacy of love, unity, and a family that had to be rebuilt from the ground up.

Chapter 11: Pages of the Past

The silence in the cottage was no longer heavy with anger, but with the quiet weight of revelation. Thandie's hand trembled as she reached for the leather-bound journal. Jay sat beside her, his gaze fixed on the note, a mixture of shame and wonder on his face. Lungie, still seated in the armchair, watched them with tear-filled eyes. The fight was over, replaced by a dawning comprehension of what their parents had truly intended.

"We should... read this together," Thandie said, her voice barely a whisper. She opened the journal to the first page, her fingers tracing the familiar handwriting.

Their parents' entries began years ago, a chronicle of their struggles. They had not been born into wealth; they had built their empire from nothing. The entries were a raw account of the sleepless nights, the difficult choices, and the constant fear of losing it all. They wrote about the guilt they felt for giving their children a life of such privilege, how they had watched their independence slowly erode.

"We've done them a great disservice," their mother had written, years before. *"The money has become a crutch. They do not know struggle, and they do not know what it is to build. We have to change this. We have to give them the one thing we truly own: the courage to be themselves, not just a reflection of our wealth."*

As they read, they learned about their parents' deliberate plan to liquidate their assets in a complex trust, not to disinherit them, but to protect the wealth from becoming a source of complacency. The letters, tied with twine, were from their father to their mother—planning this very cottage, this "thinking place" where they could come to escape the pressures of their fortune. They were a testament to their love and their shared purpose.

Then, they found entries about each of them.

"Lungie, our little creative spirit. She is the most connected to her heart, the most intuitive. But her gentle nature makes her vulnerable. We hope she finds the strength to follow her own path, without needing our constant protection."

"Jay, our brilliant, pragmatic thinker. He sees the world in numbers and logic. He will try to find a physical key, a simple answer. He has to learn that not every problem has a formulaic solution. We hope he finds a new way to see the world, and himself."

"Thandie, our fiercely independent daughter. She is a natural leader, so driven and so strong. But her pride is her armor. She will fight this battle with the law, with all her might, only to learn that her greatest strength is not in winning a fight, but in yielding to what is true."

As Lungie read the entries aloud, her voice breaking, the three siblings looked at each other, their faces streaked with tears. The anger was gone, replaced by a deep understanding and a profound sense of sadness. Their parents' final act was not one of betrayal, but one of immense love. They had not been left with a legacy of money, but with a legacy of purpose, a puzzle that could only be solved by working together.

The journal was a map to their past, a guide to their future. They had found the true inheritance. Now they had to figure out what to do with it.

Chapter 12: The Next Step

The sun was a warm, hazy orange as it began to dip below the horizon, casting long shadows across the cottage floor. The journal lay closed on the desk, its pages a testament to a love and a wisdom the siblings had never truly understood. For a long time, no one spoke. The anger that had once defined their interactions had vanished, leaving only a raw, tender silence.

It was Thandie who broke it. She reached out and touched Lungie's hand. "I'm sorry," she whispered, her voice thick with emotion. "For everything I said. For what I did."

Lungie squeezed her hand. "I know."

Jay, his head still bowed, finally looked up. He met Thandie's eyes, a silent apology passing between them. He had been so blind, so focused on the physical object of the key that he had missed the most obvious truth. He had to be the one to find the key to their parents' heart, and he had failed.

"They... they loved us so much," Jay said, his voice cracking. "They just wanted us to see it."

Lungie nodded, her gaze fixed on the journal. "We found each other," she said, quoting the final line of their mother's note. "The rest will follow. But... what's the rest?"

They looked at the journal, at the key, and at the quiet, unassuming cottage. The clues had to be here, somewhere. They began to search, not with the frantic, greedy energy of before, but with a quiet, shared purpose. They went through drawers, under cushions, and along the dusty bookshelves. But they found nothing.

“This is it,” Thandie sighed, running a hand through her hair in a rare moment of frustration. “We get it. We’re supposed to be a family. But where’s the next part of the puzzle?”

Lungie, feeling a faint chill, went back to the journal. She ran her fingers along the spine, the cover, and the worn pages. Something felt off. She stopped on one of the final pages, a page detailing their parents’ early struggles. The paper felt different, slightly thicker. She held it up to the light. On the surface, it was just a page, but a small, neat fold had been made in the bottom corner.

“Wait,” Lungie said, her voice a little breathless. “Look at this.”

Jay and Thandie crowded around her. She carefully unfolded the page, revealing a hidden compartment within the binding. Tucked inside was a smaller, folded piece of paper, weathered and faded with age. Jay carefully slid it out.

The paper held a poem in their father's hand. It was simple, almost a nursery rhyme, but its words were a puzzle:

“Where the first steps were taken, and the future was spun,

Where the old roads were broken, and the new life begun,

Find the stone in the garden, with the roots of the vine,

And know what we planted there, for this gift of ours is truly yours and truly divine.”

They read it twice, then a third time. The words were a riddle, but for the first time, they were excited by the prospect of solving it together. They looked at each other, their minds already working to decode the clues. The fighting had stopped, and a new journey had just begun.

Chapter 13: The Riddles of the Past

The three siblings sat in a tight circle on the floor of the cottage, the poem a fragile piece of history between them. The moonlight filtering through the window cast a soft, silvery glow on their faces, which were no longer etched with anger, but with a shared, focused intensity. The words of the riddle seemed to dance in the air, a final, intricate puzzle left by their parents.

"Okay, let's break this down," Thandie said, her mind already shifting into problem-solving mode. Her legal training, usually so rigid and formal, was now a tool for a much more personal kind of investigation. "'Where the first steps were taken, and the future was spun.' It has to be a place. A significant one."

Jay's brow furrowed in thought. "A place of beginning. Our first house? The little one on the hill? That's where they started the textile company, right? In the garage?"

A flicker of recognition crossed Lungie's face. "Yes," she said softly. "Mom used to call it their 'brave place.' She said it's where they truly became a family and an empire."

The mood in the room had shifted from a heavy silence to one of quiet excitement. They were a team again, for the first time in years. They packed a few things, locked the cottage, and without a word, got into Thandie's car. The drive was a world away from the silent, hostile journey of the past. They talked about their childhood, laughing at shared memories, the tension between them dissolving with every mile.

When they arrived at the old house, the sight was a jolt of nostalgia. It was no longer theirs, and a new family lived there, but the garden was still a tapestry of their memories. The same climbing vine, thick and woody, still snaked its way up the side of the garage, its tendrils wrapped around the stones of a small, forgotten path.

"The roots of the vine," Lungie whispered, her eyes wide as she pointed to a particularly large, flat stone half-buried in the soil. "The stone is right there."

Jay, ever the pragmatist, was already on his knees, his hands digging into the earth around the stone. The roots were indeed wrapped around it, as if holding it in place. With a grunt, he managed to pry it loose. Underneath, a small, rusted tin box lay hidden, looking as if it had been there for decades.

They all held their breath as Thandie carefully pried open the lid. Inside, nestled on a bed of faded velvet, was a small, ancient-looking USB drive and a single, folded piece of paper. Jay reached for the note and unfolded it, his eyes scanning the familiar, elegant handwriting.

"The family ledger," it read, in their father's neat script. *"The true accounting of our legacy. It is here, my children, where you will find what we left you, in a place we know you will find when you are truly ready."*

Chapter 14: The Final Ledger

The rusted tin box felt impossibly light in their hands as Thandie, Jay, and Lungie sat together in the car, the USB drive and the note a fragile treasure between them. The sun had set, and the journey back to the city was quiet, but it was a comfortable silence, filled with a new kind of understanding. The anger and resentment had been replaced by a shared, simmering anticipation.

"So, what do you think is on it?" Lungie finally asked, her voice hushed.

Jay gripped the steering wheel, his eyes on the road. "I have no idea. But a 'family ledger'? It has to be some sort of record of their finances. Maybe the locations of the money. I just... I can't believe we were so stupid. We were looking for a lockbox, a piece of paper, and they were talking about a computer file all along."

"They knew you would, Jay," Thandie said softly, her voice free of its usual edge. "That's what they said in the journal. They knew we would all approach it in our own way, and we had to fail on our own to come together."

The three of them made their way to Jay's apartment. It was a space they had rarely visited, as Jay's life had always seemed to be a series of business trips and work-related dinners. But now, it felt like a sanctuary. As Jay plugged the USB drive into his laptop, the siblings huddled around the screen, their hearts pounding in unison.

A folder popped up on the desktop, labeled "The Maseko Legacy." Jay clicked on it, and the screen filled with a series of sub-folders, each with a different name: "Our Story," "Our Struggles," "Our Victories," and at the very bottom, "Our Gift."

"Okay, this isn't a ledger," Jay muttered, a flicker of disappointment crossing his face.

"It is," Lungie corrected him, her hand reaching out to touch the screen. "It's their real legacy."

Thandie clicked on the "Our Gift" folder. It contained a single video file, titled "To Our Children." Jay double-clicked on it, and the screen filled with the faces of their parents, looking so much younger and more vibrant than they had in their final years. They were sitting on a couch, holding hands, their eyes bright with love.

"Hello, my dears," their mother began, her voice as warm and comforting as a blanket. "If you're watching this, it means you have finally found each other. You have put aside your differences and worked together to solve our final riddle. And that, my children, is your true inheritance."

Their father took over, his face serious. "The family ledger you sought is not a list of accounts. It is the story of how we built this life from nothing. It is a record of every failure, every lesson, and every sacrifice. We have left you not with a fortune to squander, but with the wisdom to build your own. We wanted you to see that true wealth is not something you can inherit; it is something you must create. The accounts are empty. We've given it all away."

The three of them stared at the screen, stunned into silence. Their mother smiled. "The final step of our plan is for you to decide what to do with the legacy we have given you. Do you sell everything, or do you take the knowledge we've given you and use it to build something new, together?"

The video ended, leaving the siblings staring at the blank screen. Their parents' final message wasn't a solution; it was a choice, and the hardest one they had ever faced.

Chapter 15: The Legacy of Choice

The screen went dark, and the three of them sat in stunned silence. The echo of their parents' voices hung in the air, a final, unshakeable truth that had shattered their expectations. The accounts were empty. Their inheritance wasn't a fortune, but a choice.

Jay was the first to speak, a hollow laugh escaping his lips. "It's gone," he said, shaking his head. "All of it. A lifetime of work... and they gave it all away." He looked at the USB drive in his hand as if it were a cruel joke.

Thandie, always the pragmatist, was already thinking. "They didn't give it all away, not really. They gave us the knowledge to do it ourselves. The ledger isn't a list of accounts; it's a guide. A playbook." A glint of her old legal fire returned, but this time, it was aimed at a different kind of challenge.

Lungie, however, was not focused on the practicalities. She was lost in the memory of her parents' faces on the screen, their loving smiles. "They wanted us to be together. That was the point all along. The will, the fighting, the riddles... it was all to get us to this moment, to look at each other and decide to be a family again."

The weight of her words settled over them. They saw it now, the intricate web of their parents' plan. Their mother and father hadn't just left them a problem to solve; they had left them a final act of love, a lesson that true wealth was a bond of trust.

"So, what do we do?" Jay asked, his voice soft, looking from Thandie to Lungie. The question was a loaded one, a test in itself. The option to sell the company, the house, and all their other assets and walk away with a small fortune was still there. It was the easy path.

Thandie looked at Jay, then at Lungie, a genuine smile spreading across her face. "They wanted us to build something new, together. Why would we give that up?" she said. The thought of selling seemed abhorrent now. It would be a betrayal of everything they had just gone through, a final, definitive failure.

Jay nodded, a look of resolve replacing his earlier bitterness. "We'll use the ledger. We'll learn from their mistakes and their successes. We'll start something new. Maybe... a new company. But this time, it will be our own legacy."

"A legacy of three," Lungie said, her eyes shining.

They stood together in the silent apartment, the city lights twinkling below them, a final, shared testament to their journey. The future was not guaranteed, and the path ahead was uncertain, but for the first time in a very long time, they were facing it as a team. They had lost the inheritance they thought they wanted, but they had found the one they truly needed.

Chapter 16: The Blueprint of a New Legacy

The sun rose over the city, a new day dawning not just for the world outside, but for the three siblings huddled around a coffee table in Jay's apartment. The previous night had been long, filled with shared memories, honest apologies, and the first true brainstorming session they'd had in years. The "family ledger" was open on Jay's laptop, a complex series of files documenting every triumph and failure of their parents' company.

"So, they started with one sewing machine," Lungie said, her finger tracing a blurry photo of a young, determined woman at a workbench. "They had to sell their car to buy the fabric for their first big order."

Jay, ever the strategist, was already looking at the attached spreadsheets. "Look at this. They tracked every single expense. Every penny. This wasn't just a business; it was a testament to their passion." He clicked on a folder labeled "Initial Failures," his bitterness replaced with a sense of awe. "This is priceless. We can learn from all their mistakes without having to make them ourselves."

Thandie, leaning forward with a stack of legal pads, had her own ideas. "We don't just have to pick up where they left off. We can start something entirely new. Something that reflects all of us." She looked from Jay to Lungie, a new kind of partnership forming in her mind. "Jay, you have the business sense and the connections. I can handle the legal and the contracts, making sure we build it on a solid foundation. And Lungie," she turned to her sister, her voice softening, "you have the vision.

The heart of the company. You know how to tell a story, to connect with people."

Lungie nodded, her eyes shining. The fighting felt like a distant, bad dream. The pain was still there, but it was a foundation now, not a wall. "We could do something with textiles, like they did. But... maybe with a focus on sustainable, ethical fashion. Something that gives back. Mom and Dad's legacy was about building wealth; ours can be about building a community."

Jay and Thandie both looked at her, and for the first time, a shared smile bloomed on all three of their faces. This wasn't about money anymore. It was about redemption.

They spent the next few hours sketching out a business plan on the legal pads. Jay's phone buzzed with emails from his old office, but he ignored them. Thandie's hand-written notes, once reserved for court filings, were now filled with marketing strategies. Lungie, who had always felt the most disconnected, was now the anchor of their new venture.

The sun was high in the sky when they finally paused, the apartment floor littered with crumpled paper. It was a mess, but it was their mess, and it was beautiful. The empty bank accounts no longer mattered. Their parents had given them something far more valuable: a new beginning, together.

Chapter 17: The First Stitch

The sterile scent of freshly painted concrete and the faint aroma of new fabric filled the small industrial space they had rented. It was a far cry from the opulent, wood-paneled office of their parents' company, and that was exactly the point. It was an empty canvas, a blank slate for their new beginning. Jay had found the space at a fraction of a cost, Thandie had handled the lease agreement with her usual meticulousness, and Lungie had already filled a corner with sketches and mood boards.

They were a different kind of team now. Thandie, who had once lived in a world of high-stakes litigation, now meticulously researched every potential fabric supplier, a pen poised over her legal pad as she vetted their ethical certifications. Jay, the former CFO who had negotiated multi-million dollar deals, spent his days poring over spreadsheets, but with a newfound excitement for every penny saved. And Lungie, who had always felt the most disconnected, was now the creative anchor, her touch on a sample of hemp linen more valuable than any financial forecast.

"This is it," Lungie said, holding up a swatch of a raw, undyed textile. "This is the fabric. It's durable, it's sustainable, and it feels... real."

Jay ran the fabric between his fingers, a smile on his face. "It's perfect. I just got off the phone with the supplier, a small family business. Their prices are fair, but we have to order a minimum of a thousand meters for each color. It's a huge upfront cost for us."

Thandie sighed, the old stress of a difficult negotiation returning, but this time, it was a challenge she welcomed. "That's a massive risk. We don't have that kind of capital laying around. What's the plan, Jay?"

Jay's usual cut-throat business instincts were tempered by a new sense of collaboration. He knew they couldn't just walk away. They had to make this work, together. He walked over to the whiteboard where they had scrawled their initial business plan. "Okay, so we can't afford the entire order now. But what if we don't need to? What if we start with a small, limited-run collection? We could pre-sell a certain number of pieces to fund the first order."

Thandie's eyes lit up. "A pre-order campaign. It would test the market and give us the cash flow we need. Plus, it fits with our mission of not creating waste. We only produce what people actually want to buy."

Lungie's mind was already racing with ideas for the campaign. "We can tell our story. The story of a family coming back together to create something new. Something honest. It's not just a product; it's a promise."

And so, with a shared nod, they made their first big business decision. It wasn't about leveraging their name or their parents' old contacts. It was about relying on each other, on their collective skills, and on the strength of their new, shared vision. The first stitch had been made, and the journey had truly begun.

Chapter 18: The First Sale

The final countdown was silent, shared only between the three of them in the dim light of Jay's living room. The website, designed with Lungie's earthy aesthetic and Thandie's crisp, professional copy, was a clean slate on Jay's laptop screen. It was all a leap of faith. The pre-order campaign was live, and now, all they could do was wait.

The silence stretched, heavy with the weight of their expectations. The last few weeks had been a blur of frantic activity—Lungie shooting photos of their prototypes in a small studio, Thandie crafting press releases that told their unique story, and Jay building the e-commerce platform from the ground up, his fingers flying across the keyboard with a renewed sense of purpose.

"Refresh the page?" Jay finally whispered, his voice a little hoarse.

Thandie shook her head. "Give it five minutes, at least. We just sent out the email blast."

Five minutes turned into ten, and ten into a quiet eternity. The air was thick with the anxiety that this entire, beautiful, messy plan might just fall flat. They had put everything into this—not just their time and their small savings, but their fragile, newly repaired relationship.

Then, a small, barely audible 'ping' came from Jay's laptop. His eyes, fixed on the screen, widened. "Hold on," he said, leaning in. His face, usually so composed, broke into a wide, disbelieving smile. "One. One order. We have a customer."

Thandie and Lungie shot out of their seats, rushing to his side. The screen showed a single line item: one dress, a size small, purchased. It was a single, anonymous person, somewhere in the world, who had believed in their story and their product enough to spend their money.

Lungie let out a squeal of delight, hugging Thandie and then Jay. The small number on the screen felt bigger than any fortune they could have inherited. It was validation. It was proof.

Over the next hour, a few more orders trickled in, each one celebrated with a quiet cheer. It wasn't a viral sensation, not yet. But it was momentum. A foundation. By the time the sun was fully up, they had twenty-three orders. Twenty-three strangers who were now part of their story.

They sat back on the couch, exhausted but exhilarated. Thandie leaned her head on Lungie's shoulder, a gesture that would have been unimaginable a few weeks ago. Jay closed his laptop, the screen reflecting their three tired but happy faces. The money was a good sign, but what they had truly gained was immeasurable. They had proven to themselves, and to each other, that they were capable of building something from nothing, just like their parents had. The lost inheritance was a memory; the future they were creating was now their reality.

Chapter 19: An Unexpected Visitor

The celebration had extended into the late afternoon. They had ordered food and toasted their small, but meaningful, victory with cheap sparkling cider. The glow of the laptop screen, now filled with the growing list of orders, felt warmer and more satisfying than the grandest banquet table. They were finally building something on their own terms, and the feeling was intoxicating.

The doorbell chimed, a sharp, insistent sound that shattered the easy calm of the afternoon.

"I'll get it," Thandie said, getting up from the couch. She smoothed her dress and put on her usual composed expression, a reflex from a life of dealing with unexpected solicitors.

When she opened the door, a man with a perfectly tailored suit and a slick, practiced smile was standing on the landing. It was a face she knew from countless charity events and business galas: Mr. De Villiers, a long-time associate of their father's, who had always seemed to be circling their family's empire like a shark. He had once tried to orchestrate a hostile takeover of their father's business, an attempt their mother had thwarted with surprising ferocity.

"Thandie, my dear," he said, his smile not quite reaching his eyes. "I heard a whisper that you and your siblings were starting something new. Quite the brave little venture."

Jay and Lungie, sensing the shift in the atmosphere, came to the door. Jay's hand instinctively went to Thandie's back, a silent show of support.

"Mr. De Villiers," Jay said, his voice flat. "What can we do for you?"

"I was simply checking in on the children of my old friend," he purred. "And to offer my congratulations. It's not every day one sees such initiative. The market for ethical textiles is a difficult one, however. Full of pitfalls. And competitors who don't take kindly to new players."

His gaze lingered on each of them for a moment, a veiled threat hanging in the air. "I'm sure you're aware of the resources required for a proper scaling of this business. The kind of resources your parents' company used to have." He let the implication hang. "I could be... a partner. A mentor, even. I could provide the capital and the guidance to ensure this little hobby of yours doesn't fail."

He pulled a business card from his pocket, the embossed lettering a stark contrast to their humble new venture. "Think about it. The world is a very different place without your father to protect you. A man needs allies in business, and in life."

As he turned to leave, he offered a final, unnerving smile. "I'll be watching with great interest."

The door clicked shut, but the unsettling feeling lingered. The man was a ghost of their past, a reminder of the power and money they no longer had. He wasn't just offering a partnership; he was testing their resolve. He wanted to see if they were truly different from their parents—if they could stand on their own without the wealth and influence that had once defined them. They had a shared victory, but now they had a shared enemy, too.

Chapter 20: A United Front

The silence that followed Mr. De Villiers' departure was heavier than any they had experienced before. It was a silence born not of animosity, but of shared understanding. The air, which had been buzzing with the giddy excitement of their first sales, now felt charged with a different kind of energy. He had come not to celebrate with them, but to remind them of their vulnerability.

Thandie was the first to speak, her voice low and steady. "He's not a ghost. He's a shark. And he just smelled blood in the water."

Jay walked to the door and double-checked the lock, a simple action that felt strangely significant. "He's not just testing us. He's trying to bait us. He wants us to come to him, to prove that without our parents' money, we're nothing."

Lungie, who had been listening to the conversation with an unusual stillness, spoke up. "He's wrong. We're not nothing. We're exactly what our parents wanted us to be: independent." She looked at Thandie and Jay, her eyes a mirror of their own quiet determination. "He thinks he's a part of this story, but he's not. This isn't about him or the past. This is about us and our future."

The words hung in the air, a simple truth that shifted the entire dynamic. This wasn't a battle for a lost fortune; it was a battle for their identity. Thandie, the lawyer, moved to the whiteboard and picked up a marker. "So, how do we handle this? Do we just ignore him?"

"No," Jay said, his voice firm. "Ignoring him would be a mistake. He'll see it as weakness. We need a strategy. We have to show him we're not afraid."

They began to map out a plan. Thandie's mind, once focused on the legal loopholes of a will, now worked on intellectual property rights and cease-and-desist letters. Jay's financial acumen, once used to manage a family empire, was now dedicated to securing their modest funds and seeking out investors who aligned with their values. And Lungie's creative vision was no longer just about design; it was about crafting a narrative of resilience, of a business built on ethics and passion, a story that would resonate with their customers and repel men like Mr. De Villiers.

As the sun set, casting long shadows across the room, the three of them stood shoulder-to-shoulder, a united front. They hadn't inherited a fortune, but they had inherited something far more valuable: a shared purpose and the strength to protect it. They weren't just a team; they were a family, forged in the fire of loss and rebuilt with the bricks of their own making.

Chapter 21: The Counter-Move

The whiteboard, once a blank canvas for a simple business plan, was now a complex web of flowcharts, legal jargon, and marketing slogans. They had spent the night and half the morning turning their fear into a formidable strategy. Their first target: their own vulnerability. Mr. De Villiers had tried to bait them with a lack of resources, but they were now going to show him their true resource was not money, but intellect and unity.

Thandie took the lead, her calm demeanor a sharp contrast to her ferocious focus. She drafted a series of legal documents, meticulously filing for intellectual property protection for their designs and the unique name of their brand. The process was a painstaking one, but she worked with a quiet, steady resolve. "He can't steal what's already owned," she said, her fingers flying across the keyboard. "We'll build a fortress of paperwork around our brand. So that if he tries to infringe on our work, it won't just be a moral issue—it will be a legal one."

Meanwhile, Jay, armed with his phone and his extensive network, began reaching out to a list of contacts he had compiled. These weren't the old-money titans of his father's era, but a new breed of investors—venture capitalists and philanthropists who valued a company's ethics as much as its bottom line. His pitch was simple and compelling: a family business built on a foundation of integrity and a story of resilience. He secured a few meetings, small but promising first steps that gave him a sense of purpose he hadn't felt in years.

Lungie's task was the most public. She spent hours crafting a powerful social media campaign. The message was simple: they weren't just a business, they were a testament to the power of family, second chances, and honest work. She created short videos and powerful posts that told their story, not as victims of a lost inheritance, but as creators of a new legacy. It was a narrative that resonated deeply with their customers, turning their shared vulnerability into their greatest strength.

The three of them worked tirelessly, a well-oiled machine of legal, financial, and creative power. A few days later, a small but important news item appeared in a business journal. It highlighted the siblings' new company, not as a start-up, but as a "disruptor in the ethical fashion space," built on a foundation of family and a unique, inspiring backstory. It mentioned their secured legal protections and their successful initial funding rounds. The article was a powerful public statement that they were no longer just the children of a wealthy family—they were a force to be reckoned with.

Miles away, in his opulent office, Mr. De Villiers read the article on his tablet. He had been expecting a phone call, a desperate plea for help. Instead, he was met with a bold and public declaration of their independence. He looked at the headline and a slow, grudging smile spread across his face.

"Touché," he murmured to himself, leaning back in his chair. He had expected them to crumble, but they had surprised him. They had not come to him; they had simply made it clear they no longer needed him.

Chapter 22: The Harvest

A year had passed since the day Mr. De Villiers had made his unwelcomed visit. The small cottage had long been outgrown, its walls too cramped for the vibrant chaos of a thriving business. They had moved into a light-filled warehouse in a bustling part of the city, its high ceilings and polished concrete floors a stark, modern contrast to the old workshop. The scent of fresh fabric and organic dyes filled the air, a living testament to their hard work.

Their small team had grown to a dedicated group of designers, artisans, and logistics experts. Thandie, once the meticulous lawyer, now moved with an easy authority through the business, a clipboard in her hand as she oversaw supply chains and managed their ever-expanding list of clientele. The rigid structure she had always craved was now self-built, a testament to her own design.

Jay, who had once found solace in the fleeting company of strangers and the cold logic of finance, was now a natural leader. He spent his days in meetings, not in the sterile boardrooms of old, but in bustling coffee shops and co-working spaces. He was no longer selling a name, but a story—their story—and the passion in his voice was palpable. His phone, once a tool for fleeting connections, was now a lifeline to their partners and a source of genuine excitement.

Lungie's creative vision, once confined to a few notebooks and a single machine, was now the heart of the entire operation. She was the soul of the company, her quiet passion now an open flame that inspired everyone around her. She had a new studio now, filled with natural light and fabrics of every color. She no longer just created designs; she mentored a new generation of artisans, passing on not just her skills but the spirit of their mission.

One afternoon, a delivery truck pulled away, its back doors emblazoned with their company's new logo. Thandie watched it go, a rare, unguarded smile on her face. Jay walked up to her, holding a large, steaming cup of coffee. He handed it to her without a word. Lungie came up behind them and put an arm around each of their shoulders, her touch a silent acknowledgment of the moment. They stood there, side-by-side, watching the truck disappear into the city traffic.

"Do you ever think about it?" Jay asked, his voice soft. "What if we had found it? The money?"

Thandie took a sip of her coffee, the warmth a comfort against the cool air. "I don't know," she said honestly. "But I know this is better. We built this. All of it. We didn't inherit it."

Lungie squeezed their shoulders. "Our parents gave us something more valuable than any inheritance," she said, her voice full of emotion. "They gave us each other. And a second chance to be a family."

In that moment, they didn't see the sprawling warehouse, the employees, or the thriving business. They saw the empty cottage, the tin box, and the riddle. They saw the lost, broken siblings they had once been. And they saw the family they had finally found, not in a will, but in themselves.

Chapter 23: The Final Inheritance

Three years after the day they had lost everything, Thandie, Jay, and Lungie stood side-by-side in the quiet, manicured rows of the cemetery. The same sun that had blazed on their parents' funeral now cast a gentle, golden light over the twin headstones. The marble was cool and smooth under their fingertips. There were fresh flowers on the graves, placed there by a thoughtful Lungie, their vibrant colors a testament to life and growth.

The silence this time was not heavy or hostile. It was a comfortable, shared silence, filled with the unspoken words of a long, difficult journey. They were no longer the lost, angry children from that day. Thandie's shoulders were relaxed, no longer tense with the weight of her legal fight. Jay's eyes, once so full of a cold, pragmatic anger, now held a deep, settled peace. And Lungie, whose sadness had once felt like a permanent shroud, now had a lightness in her step and a radiant smile.

"I wonder if they're proud," Lungie said softly, her voice carrying a sense of finality.

"I think they were always proud of us," Jay said, his voice quiet. "But they wanted us to be proud of ourselves, too."

"The money... it would have been a curse," Thandie said, her eyes fixed on the names etched in the stone. "It would have kept us dependent, stuck in a version of ourselves that we never had to fight for. This... this is the real inheritance. The company, the life we've built, the family we've become."

Jay reached into his pocket and pulled out a small, worn piece of paper—the note from their father. He had kept it all this time, a quiet reminder of their journey. He read the last line aloud, his voice steady. *"The true accounting of our legacy. It is here, my children, where you will find what we left you, in a place we know you will find when you are truly ready."*

He looked up, a rare, unguarded smile on his face. "He wasn't talking about the USB drive. He was talking about here." He gestured between the three of them. "He knew we'd find it when we were ready to be a family again."

The last remnants of their parents' test were finally put to rest. Thandie, Jay, and Lungie stood there for a while longer, not in sorrow, but in gratitude. They had not been left with a fortune, but with a family forged in fire. And as they walked away, hand-in-hand, they left the graveyard not as heirs to a past legacy, but as the builders of their own.

Chapter 24: A Final Legacy

Five years after they had walked away from the graves with a new sense of purpose, Thandie, Jay, and Lungie stood in the old cottage. It was no longer a place of tension and ghosts, but a home filled with warmth and the gentle hum of a new life. They had kept it, lovingly restoring it, and it had become their sanctuary—a place to return to once a year to remember where they came from and to celebrate how far they had come.

The scent of a feast cooking filled the air, a mix of spices and home-cooked warmth. Their company, "Woven Threads," had become an international success, a symbol of ethical business and beautiful design. It was a thriving, self-sufficient entity, a far cry from the small venture that had started with a few rolls of fabric and a handful of notebooks.

Jay, the ever-so-disciplined financial mind, now had a relaxed demeanor, his laughter coming more easily. He had found a new, quieter kind of peace, a peace that wasn't reliant on spreadsheets or stock portfolios, but on the simple pleasure of working alongside his siblings. He was no longer just a money man; he was a leader, a partner, and most importantly, a brother.

Thandie, whose life had once been defined by rigid formality, was a force of creative and legal prowess. She was now expecting her first child, her fierce determination transformed into a gentle, protective energy. The legal battles she once sought were no longer a source of stress, but a wellspring of wisdom that she used to protect their growing company, her family, and the legacy they were building.

And Lungie, the sensitive soul of the family, had become a renowned designer. Her intuitive sense of style had made their company a household name. She was no longer living in her parents' shadow, but was the source of a vibrant, inspiring light. She had found a new kind of creative power—one that came from the joy of building something from the ground up, not just from a place of grief.

The three of them sat around a simple wooden table, the same one where they had once so bitterly argued. Now, it was laden with food, wine, and laughter. They raised their glasses, the clinking of the glass a soft, melodic sound.

"To Mom and Dad," Thandie said, her voice thick with emotion. "For giving us the greatest lesson of all."

"They didn't leave us an inheritance," Jay added, his eyes sparkling. "They gave us the chance to earn one."

Lungie smiled, tears of joy welling in her eyes. "They gave us each other," she whispered.

And in that moment, in the quiet heart of the cottage, they realized the true legacy their parents had left behind. It wasn't money. It wasn't land or titles. It was the enduring, unbreakable bond that had been forged in the fire of loss. They were no longer the heirs to a fortune, but the keepers of a new legacy—one built on resilience, love, and the unshakeable foundation of family.

Book Dedication

For the one who believed in this story from the very beginning.

For every word written and every challenge overcome. This is for you.

For myself, who learned that some legacies are not inherited, but are built on one page at a time...

Author's Acknowledgements

To myself:

This book is a testament to my perseverance. Thanks to me for showing up at the page, day after day, when the words were hard to find and the plot felt tangled. Thanks for listening to the characters, for believing in their story, and for having the courage to share it with the world. You took a spark of an idea and turned it into a complete world, and for that, you deserve all the credit.

This journey taught me that the real reward is not in the final product, but in the growth and dedication required to create it. I have built a new legacy, not just in this book, but in myself.

Thanks for seeing it through to the end.

ABOUT AN AUTHOR

Sibongiseni Masengemu is a storyteller at heart, with a passion that spans both the vivid world of fiction and the compelling realm of non-fiction. A writer of diverse interests, he is also a lover of the romance genre. His unique approach to narrative is deeply rooted in history, where he finds inspiration to create new laws and concepts based on true stories. He believes that the most profound lessons and the most powerful narratives are often hidden in the legacies we leave behind. Through his work, he aims to explore the intricate tapestry of human relationships, the complexities of inherited legacies, and the ultimate power of self-determination.

Don't miss out!

Visit the website below and you can sign up to receive emails whenever Sibongiseni Masengemu publishes a new book. There's no charge and no obligation.

https://books2read.com/r/B-A-LADUC-ZDZVG

BOOKS 2 READ

Connecting independent readers to independent writers.